ndakinna

NDAKINNA
(Our Land)

New and Selected Poems

Joseph Bruchac

WEST END PRESS

Acknowledgments

The international small press and literary magazine movement has been an important part of my life for more than thirty years. When I look back over the list of presses and literary magazines where many the poems in this collection first appeared, I am struck by the generosity and the courage shown by those editors and publishers whose aims were never financial profit and whose hearts were always much larger than their pocketbooks. Some of these magazines and presses no longer exist, but like stones that fall into the water, their ripples are still touching distant shores. As we say in the Abenaki language, *Ktsi wliwini nidobak*. Thank you, my friends.

Bamboo Ridge for "Seeing the Whales"
Calapooya Collage for "Moccasin Flowers"
Gatherings for "Routine Check"
Groundswell for "Let the Midnight Special"
The Guadalupe Review for "Turning from the Klan"
Lake Effect for "Forest Fire From the Air"
Lips for "Walking at Night in Slade Brook Swamp"
Nexus for "The Guachero Bird Cave"
Okike for "Crossing into West Germany"
The Pennsylvania Review for "The Flint from Missisquoi"
The Pittsburgh Quarterly for "Before the Quake"
Poems from the Earth for "Transplanting Trees"
Poets On for "To See the Deer"
Red Dirt for "Matsinad Namas"
Snail's Pace Review for "The Baux"
Tonantzin for "Ndakinna" and "Wawanolewad"

"An Abenaki Song of the Stars," "Ktsi Wadzo," "Walking at Night in Slade Brook Swamp," "Mannigebeskwas," and "The Spreaders" from *Langes Gedachtnes und Andere Gedichte/Long Memory and Other Poems*, published by OBEMA Bilingual Editions, Osnabruck, Germany, 1989.

"Walking in November Across the Stream to the Sweat Lodge," "Walking at Night With My Son, James," "Birch Island at Dawn in August," "At the old Dog's Grave," and "Tangled Lines" from *Walking With My Sons*, Landlocked Press, Madison, Wisconsin, 1986.

First edition, October 2003
ISBN: 0-9705344-7-7

Photographs by Joseph Bruchac
Canoe with bear and butterfly by Aaron York
Book and cover design by Nancy Woodard

West End Press • P.O. Box 27334 • Albuquerque, New Mexico 87125

Contents

Wli Dogo Wôngan:
For All My Relations

I. NDAKINNA (Our Land)

AN ABENAKI SONG OF THE STARS

Dancing, dancing
dancing we sing
there was never a time
when we were not dancing

the sacred hoop
the drum of the earth
throbs beneath us
circling our steps

there are hunters here
here the animals too
know the sacred breath
rising from the earth

we stars are the rain
held in clouds of heaven
call and we will come dancing,
great and small come dancing

dancing, dancing
we have always been dancing
dancing above your dreams

KTSI WADZO

There is a place
I have often seen,
more real than this room
or the pen in my hand.
I go there by passing
through valleys which sing,
the way lined by great pines,
wiping my brow in fever.

The place is a mountain.
I have seen it.
Rising over our town,
it was shaped of clouds.

At times I forget
that shining mountain.
Many years go by,
all of my old people
and their understanding
gone back into earth,
then that place
finds me again
and the ground begins
once more to softly
drum their footsteps.

I go walking
through those valleys
which ring like bells.
I climb that mountain,
lift my feet
and find I am flying.

Speaking of it now,
I know I will return.
When I hear it call,
I will rise and go.

Someday, perhaps,
my own two sons
will hear my voice,
part of the song
from a shining mountain
which circles
into their dreams.

Ktsi Wadzo: "Big Mountain."

WALKING IN NOVEMBER ACROSS THE STREAM TO THE SWEAT LODGE
In memory of Sam Ray

The leaves fallen
from the creekside maples
no longer blaze as red as embers.

Earth brown, they close
like fists around
their own lives,
loosening into soil.

My red dog grabs a stick in her mouth,
so long it knocks against the trees
as she runs up the narrow path,
making a music which startles, delights her.

No great issues this morning,
no more to do than burn tobacco,
speak words by the fire pit,
strip the blankets from the sweat lodge.

One old quilt has become as thin as paper.
I laugh as I lift it—the white-footed mice
have stolen the batting to weave into nests.
Light shines through its patterns
of red and orange, a sudden flower.

Walking back, the wind against my face,
I am suddenly wreathed in clouds of breath.

There is no way to count
the blessings of seasons,
the fallen leaves.

WALKING AT NIGHT IN SLADE BROOK SWAMP

Western Abenaki children were often told stories
about The Swamp Dweller, a woman whose voice
was sweet as she called children to lure them into
places where they might become lost and would
drown. The Penobscot called her "The Jug Woman."

The tracks in the snow
are not my own
although they follow my feet

the darkness which fills them
after I have passed
is colored by memories
deeper than I have stepped

when I break through
the bone of ice
the water beneath is warmer
from the remembering sun
of something left behind

here in this place
neither woods nor lake

here where the ancient dangerous voice
of something neither inhuman nor human
is almost sweeter than the mesmeric tones
of bright light machines that promise
all in a world where all is death

the jug-woman calls
back into the alder thickets
back through the strew of tamarack needles
to the place where earth falls away
beneath me and I will be lost
lost as my ancestors were lost.

Whose face am I wearing
in this cycle
although I know
whose spirit I carry?

For this I choose
to walk darkness' edge
to make my own voice
sweeter than danger
sweeter than hers
this time as I call her

Old Woman, come out
of that place where you hide,
learn to feed now on something
more than our dying
this time, Old Woman,
we need to walk forward.

MANNIGEBESKWAS

*Mannigebeskwas is a spirit being who lives alone in the deep forest.
She is the embodiment of the independence of Abenaki women.*

When your people see me
walking in the forest
they know my name
by the distance I keep
between myself
and any mother who would scold me,
seeing me as I am now,
hair uncombed and tangled
with new green leaves,
clothes stained by berries
as I lift up handfuls
of the ripest fruit
to let the juice
trickle from my laughing mouth.
Sun-warmed moss
beneath my back,
limbs open to sky's caress
on the slope of the shining mountain,
I drink cold rain
and taste the seasons.
No man can keep me
tied to his puny fire.

The animal people know me best.
My voice is true
as their own musics.
My fingers are strong
to comb the burrs
from the great bear's fur.
Some nights I sleep
with my sisters, the wolves,
curled into their white breath.

Now you, who have seen me
as I sometimes walk
when it pleases me to do so,
with the grace I've been given
by the deer, erect as the ash tree,
long limbs clean and strong,
my hair combed neatly,
my clothing new, my face glowing
with something you do not understand,
you say you have conceived love for me.
You play your courting songs
at the clearing's edge,
sweeten your breath
through a cedar flute.

Be thankful I am not one of those
who calls young men into darker places,
leads them into dangers,
laughs at their despair.

Go ahead, play your song
if it pleases you
and I may just listen
if it touches the spirit.

But I stay with no man.
Before dawn comes again
I will rise and go,
travel over the mountains,
teaching each bird its song.

THE SPREADERS

There were various local spirits of which Abenaki hunters had to beware. Among these were "The Spreaders," who lived near a campsite avoided by most travellers along the St. Maurice River in Quebec. Anyone who stayed there might wake up in the morning with their eyes and mouth propped open with sticks, their fingers and toes spread apart.

We came back to hunt here only
a few seasons, old folks say.
It was 1840 when Piel
was found like that, and
two years later when Sosap
turned up missing
we found him along
the river bank wedged
between tree roots
where he'd pulled himself,
wriggling like a caterpillar.

We had lived long enough
to forget old stories
about this place, the anger
of those whose grounds were defiled
by hunters who failed
to hang up the skulls
of beaver they trapped,
to use all of each animal
and burn the rest,
to keep the game happy.

Eyes open, mouth wide,
fingers splayed
like a spider's web,
skin stretched to the tearing point
by sharp splinters of ash.

Bones were the warning
long ago to those
who came too close
to this unforgiving place—
brittle fingers, grey as dead twigs,
legs wide and disjointed,
arms out like wings.

We sit, propped up,
throats dry, trying to swallow,
to say the vowels lips cannot grasp,
HIIIIEEEE HAAAEEEEEYYY
as the Spreaders watch.
Eyes cold, they sharpen
more sticks, flex webbed hands
knowing their sleep charms
will relax our fears
till eyes open to a light
from which we cannot turn.

FIRE SAND

Walking through the woods
on an autumn morning
I come to the circle
where we had our last fire
where twigs and logs
gave up their shape
to return the heat of sun
to the air.

Bending, I lift a handful of ashes,
skwedaibegwi, fire sand, we call it,
new earth formed by fire,
grey as sky before dawn.
As it sifts through my fingers,
a small wind takes it
and it dances that same
flowing dance
which the young trees know
with their supple branches,
a dance which always ends
with the earth.

The fire sand falls
between my fingers,
eager to return to the soil,
to join once more
the roots of the trees,
to lift once again
and reach up for the sun.

WAWANOLEWAD

For Chief Homer St. Francis,
descendent of Grey Lock

They saw the mountains
held in northern mist,
larger than the eyes of greedy men

They said, this place
shall be our refuge,
we shall follow these rivers
upstream with the salmon
we shall sleep with the Grandmother Bear
in these hills and these caves

Those who follow as friends
they will find our hands open
those who follow to fight
shall find our fists closed
on our bowstrings

We will be here
as certain as dawn
on the high peak,
where the snow
is a mantle, vanished
out of the sight
of those who would hunt us
like the breath of the deer
in the shadowy cedars.

Wawanolewad: he who throws others off the track

MATSINAD NAMAS

Silver eyes turned to silt
they lie in the pool
of stagnant water.
Wading in, I cup them
scales whispering light,
a minnow, black-lined,
stiff as a pencil,
two fingerling trout
their sides red as fire.

I might have saved them
had I come sooner,
carried them back
to spring headwaters.
But my good intentions
can lend them no breath.

Leaving them at water's edge
where they will be found
by the raccoons, the flies,
I remember the teaching
that nothing is wasted
when it is left
to touch the earth.

At James Bay, though,
half this continent north,
Cree people eat fish
filled with mercury,
from plants which trade
native lives for power.
And only a dozen
miles downstream from here
the Hudson River's bed is dark
with chemicals whose names
spell out death.

Today
I pray
that when my time comes
to give up breath
may my own flesh
carry little
of civilization,
let it find
new life in death.

  Matsinad Namas: "Dead Fish."

OGEMAKW

My great grandfather pounded ash
stripped of its bark,
the withes split free
into splints he plaited into baskets,
then took down the hill to Saratoga,
sold to summer people on the easy porches
of big hotels in the season of horses.

His own horses were heavy-chested,
slower-footed than those which circled the tracks.
Their bones circled back into our earth
around this farm where unused fields
have returned to locust and to sumac,
to oak and maple, to birch and pine,
and on some hills, where the right seeds fell,
ash trees tall enough this year to cut
into man-long logs for basket-making.

Most cut ash today for heat,
always the best of burning trees,
its wood a premium trucked down
in face cords from our thinning forests.

But my family knew ash
as they knew their own flesh.
The ancient story tells
of how Gluskabi pierced the trunk
of the straightest ash with his arrows
and the Abenaki stepped forth strong,
their hearts as green and growing as ash,
their feet always remembering the soil.

I've made few baskets with my hands,
though I know the weave
of strip between strip,
to split the 12th to make 13
(the same number as Abenaki nations),
to bind the top bending over withes,
to dive in and out like a fish through waves,
making a pattern the sweetgrass learns
when plaited by summer wind
and I have walked above the seasons
when winter has covered this earth
with his blanket, held up
by the web of bear paws shaped
by old Sabbatis' knowing hands.

The house where I was raised
stands on Splinterville Hill,
named for those who made baskets,
knew the white ash and black ash,
the way to use the winged seeds for tonic,
how the chewed inner bark
is a poultice for sores,
how the small branches can be
bent and shaped into snowshoes,
lacrosse sticks and tools.

Whenever they peeled ash limbs each spring
they saw that its pale flesh was clean
as the hearts of those who remember
the circling weave of roots into our land.

> *Ogemakw*: the white ash tree. Literally translated
> the word means "snowshoe tree."

FOUR POEMS FOR NDAKINNA

1.

As we drove north
the land told us stories,
the shapes of mountains
remembered Odziozho,
and an old man poled
his flat bottomed boat
at the edge of the lake
back four hunded years
where trees lift like arrows
and the trapping is good.

Seven decades ago,
No one here called them Indians.
They kept their names
hidden within words they spoke
to each other or in silences
they gave to all faces not Abenaki.

Frenchmen, gypsies, the older names
were changed from Sabattis to St. Baptiste,
from Bonsawinno, "keepers of the sacred fire,"
to Bowman, those who hide their arrows.

2.

Near that town where the lake
is like a wide meadow
the birds flocked in great numbers,
the fishing was good,
the mud right for making pots,
the willows supple to bend into frames.
There a whole village of people lived
still in the age
when stone speaks with a voice.
Their canoes were silent over the water,
their eyes kept distant
from the shops and the streets.

But the local fathers
called them thieves and gypsies,
said they were smugglers, passing too freely
up this lake beyond boundaries
named into a nation.
The Great War began
and for lack of Germans
or other imported enemies to fear,
they decided the gypsies by the water
were the closest danger.

One night the good citizens
of the town came down
on the encampment, circled
it with torches
and the steel of guns.
The men and women
in their clothes of deerskin
were loaded into the backs of the trucks,
taken off into an American darkness
and never seen again.
The children, those young
and pale-skinned enough
to learn, were given
to other families to raise
up as good U.S. citizens.

3.

In the new Tribal Council Office,
an old railroad station
bought for a dollar
from Canadians,
the chief sits behind the desk
where he's waited for us,
late up the winding roads.
Not a healer, but a man who listens,
he knows when to joke
as we talk of deer and trapping,
leading our voices towards
the land which claims us,
his eyes always looking
just a little deeper
into mine, into John's,
remembering the names of places
written history hasn't found yet.

4.

There in the bay
below Burlington town,
just past the islands
where the bears swim across
is the island called Rock Dunder.

People pull up their cars here,
look out past the harbor,
tasting the first of spring in the air.

Some boys one summer
saw a bear swimming out
from mainland to island.
They decided to kill it,
rowed way out,
swung their paddles
from the boat
at its sealslick head.
But the bear ducked the blow,
climbed in over the side,
sat in the bow of the boat,
and then growled.
"Whatever you want,"
the boys said to the bear,
then rowed him the rest
of the way to his island.

The other older name for Rock Dunder
is Odziozhen—"The Guardian's Rock."
A few yards wide, a few yards long,
it belongs to the Abenaki people,
for long ago it was Odziozho.
When he made this land
in the form it is now,
he dragged his heels to shape the streams,
scooped up the hills with his palms.
The last thing, they say,
that he made was this lake—
Petonbowk, "The Waters in Between."
This looks good, he said,
I think I'll stay here.
Then he shaped himself
into a rock and sits there still
in the mouth of the bay.

Come close to Odziozhen
and you see that its surface
is alive with life, moss and lichen
and insects swarm in great numbers
and all around it the water
seems to glow as if a light
shone from under the surface.

That's the way it was
a long time ago,
that's the way it is today.

LOOKING FOR A NAME FOR THIS DAY

I see the red-tail hawk come low
circling from the east, then rising
towards the north
where a hundred geese V'd,
following the old trail
of their ancestor's voices
into a spring wind.

Two black ducks, a female
and her mate fly,
wings whistling
through the high branches
of the old basswood tree
at the edge of the woods
where a woodpecker's
staccato search for insects
carves the face of his hunger,
makes the holes in a branch
which a boy will find tomorrow
and turn into the first flute.

THE FLINT FROM MISSISSQUOI

The white stone broke free at my touch.
I carry now its edges with me.
On one side there are brown tracings—
roads drawn on the earth far below,
the dark circling signs of water,
travels I've made and not understood,
future distances shaping my feet.
On the other side, black dots of lichen,
dry, seemingly without life,
yet holding on, even to the stone,
holding closer than flesh to bones,
seen only by those who place their faces
close to the earth, those who are tired,
those who have been pressed down,
those who hide there, rest there,
gather an older strength and wait.
The shape of the stone, flint flaked
by the hammer of seasons, is almost
that of an arrowhead, part of Odziozho's flesh,
I see it in flight, striking the tree,
making new people with old eyes,
their skins paler, but their hearts
knowing the song of wind through ash leaves
in a coming spring.

MOCCASIN FLOWERS

I dug small fingers into earth
still gritty with cinders
fifty years after the heat
of fire which ate
the house great-grandparents built.

I was putting in a moccasin flower
brought in a thick bundle
of green-mossed soil
from the right-of-way
staked by the state
straight through our land—
trying to save what I could
before bulldozers came.

But as I grubbed down
something smooth and cool
bit the tips of my fingers.
I pulled my hands back,
thin coils of blood
red as the hunger
of a white man's fire
crawled down into my palms.

Forty years later,
I still hold those scars
and that green shard
of glass sharp-edged and melted
in that ancestral blaze
the Hayes boys set
to sear away
our names from this soil
my grandfather held,
building another foundation of stone
on earth memoried with ash.

Sometimes, in spring,
as cars roar past,
the brilliant green
of a long-veined leaf
sprouts near old stones.
The shape of its blossom
is that of a foot
which leaves no tracks,
but journeys on
in spite of it all,
towards new generations.

FIRST HOEING

The point of the hoe edges between
green spears of corn, circling
each new hill with loose soil
to hold roots for tall growth,
cut away shoots of grass
and the tangle of bindweed.

My back feels the old ache
bending into the hoe,
yet each time I reach further
till warmth washes through muscles.

This hoe was my grandfather's.
I am taller than he
and must bend more to grasp
it as close to this land
which he held with such ease.
From my small height
I can still see no further
into soil than he saw
as he cared for his friends,
the Three Sisters of life,
the Corn, Beans and Squash.

The bird songs which I hear
are the same ones he knew,
and as I hold his hoe,
so the new generations
of small animals circling
their seasons around mine—
the rabbit and raccoons,
the moles and the woodchucks—
are part of an old pattern,
not war but a balance
of feeding and giving birth.

So I grasp this hoe,
not as some hold a gun,
for there are no real
enemies on this earth.
I hold it, instead,
as a part of myself,
a longer arm, a sharper finger
to point myself
through this time of labor,
through growth.

TO SEE THE DEER

We'd drive towards the dawn
along those winding roads,
cross the Hudson at Schuylerville
leaving behind the Battlefield Monument
none of us ever climbed.
We'd pass before first light
through Greenwich and Cambridge,
turning always towards the sun.
We'd go until the roads grew thin
then stop at last in Vermont,
a border shaped by one gesturing hand.
There the old man would point
towards shapes on a hill,
stones which lifted heads into life,
grey as that late autumn sky
before touched by first light.

We'd leave our car
to watch them grazing
as the morning sky began
to remember the colors of day.

Wild brothers and sisters,
their gaze turned from our eyes,
their senses caught all of our presence.
We had come without guns,
come only to see
and they, ones owned most by this land,
allowed us to watch them,
slow steps sure, full of grace.

Earth all around was open to them,
the field once cleared
returning the brush,
the old enduring wildness
regaining its place again
when left alone just a handful of seasons.

That was the message
the old man gave me,
a story without words
for my memories to read.
Now decades after
his return to earth
my own slow, overcivilized mind
has finally, it seems, begun—
slow as the spread of morning sun
across autumn clouds—
to understand.

WALKING AT NIGHT WITH MY SON, JAMES

This summer he's grown to my own height.
Our shoulders almost touch as we walk,
flashlights dark, the path through the field.
We remember old games, knowing night by touch
rather than going, like tightrope walkers,
on a thin beam of light from one hand to the earth.

The moon is a golden apple sliced in half
by shadow, glazed by southern clouds.
We pause where the meadow grass is highest,
both stopped by the thick smell of campion blossoms.
They're all around us, my son says, look!
Their blossoms are like larger, paler stars
in the sky spread at our feet.

So we stand for a time, shoulders almost touching,
in the midst of this field off the Middle Grove Road,
in the midst of our lives, sharing late August darkness.
All around us night flowers.

BIRCH ISLAND AT DAWN IN AUGUST

For Jesse

My son's paddle
thumps the canoe
as he circles the island.
It sounds a note
like a deep wooden drum.

A small wind begins to rise,
cuts the thin smoke
of a fire rekindled
from last night's ashes.

The fox sparrow,
galaxies in its eyes,
hops closer to the clearing edge
as if trying to be
a thing of land again
though nervous wings
reclaim it for the sky.

Writing these words
I follow that rhythm,
taste smoke swirled by wind,
spin in the reflection of flight
in a small bird's wings.

Yet, even as that drumbeat fades,
I know my silence separates us.
We are close yet distant,
tied by ancient bonds
like the lake's clear waters
and that mystic union
of hydrogen and oxygen
which throbs life through my veins.

I put down my pen
and the poem ends.
But the drum beat continues,
the slow widening orbit
of sons from fathers
like dawn from old darkness
goes on.

AT THE OLD DOG'S GRAVE

The neighborhood children have placed flowers
on the mound of sand near the wood's edge.
As we walk the path which her dark feet
led us along so many times
I pick a bloodroot, that first spring flower
which still holds the snow in its petals.
Red sap flows from the stem.
I use it to mark lines beneath our eyes,
to guide them towards both sunset and sunrise.

Sitting, we talk of those three parts
our old people knew—that body which must go
back to the earth, that spirit within
every living thing, a gift which returns
to creation the way waters go back to sun,
that guardian soul which will watch us now,
touching our memories, guiding in dreams.

My older son on whose bed she slept
turns his anger away from the ants
he has seen on her grave.
They are only messengers
carrying the news of her flesh
to the roots of small grasses.

We laugh then at the thought
of her spirit standing,
stiff-legged and barking
as my father dug the grave,
not yet realizing she was dead,
killed by the car she did not see
while we were away.
She always saved that bark for him,
the smell of his hands from a thousand animals
and sixty years of tanning deerskins.

Before we leave, we link our hands,
let her old soul lead us—as it led her
away from weakening spine, eyes going blind—
back into the cycle which strengthens hearts
part of each other, part of everything which lives.

WHITETAIL BUCK ON THE DANIELS ROAD

I saw its eyes before I saw the deer.
The sun was gone, a red glow in the west.
It was that time when everything seems near,
just setting out when most move towards rest.
Its path was certain as an open chart
and what I started would have been its end,
the thump of metal stilled its pounding heart
and left another wound for time to mend,
my speed exacting silence as its price
had not I slowed already for that power
of daylight vanishing, the slow release
of light to shadow, evening's crimson flower.
And so I stopped—perhaps it saw my face
before it leaped and left me praising grace.

SOUTH GREENFIELD ROAD

October 1984

The smell of tobacco,
burning leaves,
the cold morning air
outside the Greenfield Post Office
as an old man in a beach jacket,
cloth cap and khaki work pants
crosses from the Town Hall,
walks with that walk
of old men back from
a life in the woods,
the same walk a bear walks
toes out, waddling
along the potholed edges
of the South Greenfield Road.

Down that road, on the farm
once my Slovak grandfather's,
a grey horse is running
through the small field
where my grandmother hoed the corn.
She carried her sorrow
wrapped in a cloth
above her forehead.
When her daughter died
in 1945, flown home
her limbs thin
from the fevers of the Philippines,
Grandma Bruchac said she would never
cut her hair again.
In her seventies
it hung down, in the mornings,
 fine and grey as the mist
above the creek, flowed
far past her waist,
then was tied into a tight bun,
held tightly, hidden as the old stories
spoken in a strange tongue of shame.

Once again the abandoned children,
their father lost in a steel mill,
suckle the teats of a great bear.
A marvelous fish
enters the room, stands in front
of the Philco's screen,
offers a trinity of wishes.
And the dead rise at the touch
of a blessed cross,
the faces of the Virgin
are held above the old brass bed
in a light streaming
across an ocean
from a window in Bratislava.

The old man goes into
the Post Office,
and the road closes
once more to my eyes.
The door swings as I pass through
into another turn of season,
the sway of the wings of geese
far above us, whispering
down past the old Kaydeross Range
where the bear whose clan
holds the eyes of both sides of my blood
grumbles in the thin branches
of an abandoned apple tree,
mouthing half-bitter fruit.

BOBCAT, 1953

Back arched like a question mark,
gaze steady on mine,
the bobcat backed out of the tangle
slow paws silent on needles.

My Indian grandfather said
Don't too many
sneak up on a bobcat,
but if they do
it's an easy shot.
They got
too much pride
to just turn and run.

I remembered that
as the bobcat's eyes turned
away from mine,
seeing those whose names
knew how to hide,
blending once again
into shadow, cedar and pine.

TANGLED LINES

In memory of my father, Joseph Bruchac

The boat began to drift with the wind
which whipped down Deer Pond,
turned us against the anchors.

The loon which danced
all the way from the point
beside us dove and was gone.

White lines drifting
in long lazy S's
down into the hemlock water
tightened and ran
as trout after trout
took hooks fast
as we could rebait.

Anchor ropes twisted,
trout braiding our lines,
hats blown off down the pond,
my father and I leaned back and laughed

as he laughs today
from his stiff bed
where pale tubes drift
to intravenous racks
and the EKG monitor sketches
green peaks and depths
of his pulse and breath.

I was just there again, he says.
*Remember that day—the loons
and the wind?* And though his hand
is cool in mine, I laugh with him,
tangling our lines into memory.

A SONG OF FALLING SNOW

For Peter Kinne
Berkshire School,
January 1990

A sound comes
out of the forest
as it fills with falling snow

It is my father's voice
and it is a song
although I never heard him sing
even in dreams in the years
since he has been gone

I am going now
to walk in that forest
to gather the many words
falling white on my shoulders.

DIGGING

Sometimes the spade
glides down into sand
the weight of your body
riding it in as easy
as a spoon into sugar

but beneath the soil
one can never tell
what waits for the point
of deliberate metal
to turn its course, or
hold it tight

sometimes a stone
shivers like the nerve
in a tooth
through your bones
vibrating your back
like a tuning fork
the steel of the tool
screeking like new chalk
drawn across a blackboard

sometimes a root
and the edge chunks, sticks
and you feel a life
holding back, holding on
as you lever it free,
lift it up and then stab
the blade down
like a bullfighter
making the kill

but whatever is there,
to dig down takes its toll,
makes hands callous, backs stiffen
and into your arms
the heaviness of the earth you displace
will settle as the day grows thinner

whatever you dig
whatever is hidden
will be seen in your eyes.

A FISHING STORY

For more than sixty springs Old Bill
fished Bell Brook from its spring-fed source
in the deer-tracked swamp near the Greenfield Mobil
down to where it widens by the Stewart's Plant.
His old pick-up parked along 9N,
I'd see him edging towards the culvert
above the Brook View Trailer Park
to drop his line in every morning
after heavy rains swelled up the waters
luring lunker trout up the feeder stream.

Later on, mid-morning, his eyes a-squint
against the sun on the Town Store stoop,
he'd sort out his mail and the morning's gossip,
ready to tell whoever would listen
about the fourteen-inch squaretail trout
he'd just snaked out from under the road.

Then, one spring when I was getting lumber
from Loeffler's Mill along the brook,
Herb shook his head as he totalled me up.
"Hear about Old Bill? The Doctor cut
his whole foot off at the ankle—sugar.
Guess he won't be poundin' Bell Brook any more."

Two weeks later, though, there was that truck
parked on the shoulder and Old Bill limping
on his new metal foot, pole in his hand
drawing him on down to the healing water
where he kept on fishing three more years
until he passed away last winter.

I fish that brook, too, but for years
I left that culvert for Bill to fish,
the weeds beat flat along the bank
where he always stood, inching, inching
his forty pound nylon into the ripple.

That first spring, though, after Bill's death
in the Moon when the Frogs Sing, I couldn't resist.
The sun was just up, a single wood duck
winging over the road into the swamp.
Pole in my hand, I crept to the edge.
But before I could drop a worm in that spot
where the current cuts beneath the bank,
something bigger than any trout swam out.
Its fur was slicked back in a certain way
like thin grey hair round an old man's face.
It looked up at me, then it was gone
back underwater and into the culvert.

I reeled in my line and went back up the bank.
That place wasn't mine to fish that day.
But I smiled as I thought of how that old muskrat,
escaped from the trap of a winter past,
swam so smooth with one missing back paw.

SWEAT LODGE BY BELL BROOK

Crossing the stream,
pooled waist-deep
against piled rocks
lifting above the surface
like the knees of old men,
the bridge of boards
salvaged from the old house
bends under my weight,
but it does not break.

Yellow jewelweed bobs
against my bare chest
leaving orange pollen
streaking my skin
as I climb the small hill
and enter the clearing.

The fire pit has cooled,
the sand of ashes
spread like Grouse's tail.
Pitted lava stones
from the southwest sit
in a quiet circle
about the pit, like elders
waiting for the council
to begin again.

Logs of cedar and pine,
of ash and dry elm
are split and stacked,
waist high, prepared
to rekindle again
the heat of our elder
brother the sun.

The sweat lodge
faces the east,
twelve peeled poles
bent and tied
to form a small dome
like that of the sky,
large enough to hold
the prayers
of seven men.
Soon, in sacred darkness,
the water will sing
on the stones
as I bend close to earth
and thank all my relations.

TRANSPLANTING TREES

First dig the hole
where it will go
wide enough for roots,
deep enough for growth.

Fill the hole with water,
let it seep into sides,
earth drinking her fill
to share with a new guest.

Trench around the tree
to be transplanted,
a circle wide
as its spread of branches.

Remember that evergreens
always root shallow
while hardwoods drive taproots
down close to their height.

Wrap a sack, tied
to keep the ball of soil intact
holding root hairs finer
than mist unbroken.

Do this all near the time
of first or last frost,
just when earth is waking
or drifting towards rest.

When you transplant trees,
you renew an old trust,
making room for new branches
to shade us with peace.

WINTER FIRE

Snow
is deep
around the lean-to.

The firestick
spins
a bright eye
out of cedar,
a red coal
which breathes
with my breath,
flows smoke
then lifts
up into flame.

Small sticks
tipi-shaped
begin to remember
an ancient tongue,
the language
of burning,
bright words
borrowed from
the sun.

Heat melts
the snow into a circle.

I lean
into its warmth
my hands
held out
like those
of a priest

But this sacrament,
this winter blessing
of life
is one
which I receive.

NDAKINNA

You cannot understand
our land with maps
lines drawn as if earth
were an animal's carcass
cut into pieces, skinned,
divided, devoured —
though always less eaten
than is thrown away.

See this land instead
with the wind eagle's eyes,
how the rivers and streams
link like sinew through a leather garment
sewed strong to hold our people,
patterns of flowers
close to the brown soil.

Do not try to know
this land by roads,
hard lines ripped
through old stones,
roads which still
call for blood
of not just those who cross,
wild eyes blinded
by twin suns startling the night,
but also those who seek to follow
the headlong flow
atop that dark frost
unthawed by the sun—
though seasons and
the insistent lift
of the smallest seeds
seek, without ceasing,
space for the old soil.

Instead, let your feet
caress this soil
in the way of the deer
whose feet follow and form
trails through the ways
of least resistance,
knowing ridges and springs,
ways of wind
through the seasons,
the taste of green twig
and tender grass,
the sweet scent of rain
urged up from moist earth.

When you feel this land
when you taste this land
when you hold this land
as your lungs hold your breath

you will be the rattlesnake
always embracing earth with her passage,
you will be the salmon, a chant
whipped through the ripple,
you will be the deermouse,
small feet stitching the night,
you will be the bear,
thunder held in soft steps,
when your songs see this land
when your ears sing this land
you will be this land
you will be this land.

II. TRAVELING STORIES

THE WHITE DOG

At a library conference in Chicago
one woman spoke, tears
at the edge of her words,
of how the animals all are dying.
Now, no more than a heartbeat later,
I find myself in an airplane
and I do not know how
I have come so far.

Oil surges from the wounded tundra,
stiff wings cut like razors through sky,
but, somehow, as I close my eyes
I see a certain small darkened room
at Onondaga and I know
just beyond that curtain
the carved basswood faces
of our Grandfathers wait,
hold their knowing gazes
towards that ancient circle
which was tomorrow yesterday.

In that room, my hands touched
the white dog, the last one
at Onondaga, born to carry
up to Our Creator the messages
of prayer and smoke.

Its eyes were bright as glass,
reflecting my face and all around me,
and its stiff taxidermied limbs
held the stance of a guardian.

As I saw the white dog, I saw this day
two decades since then, a whisper of breath
asking us to take one path or the other,

a choice which we must make again,
for even from this diminished spring
waters may deepen and again
be sweet for seven generations.

THE GUACHERO BIRD CAVE

Asa Wright Preserve, Trinidad

The varying call of the cocoa thrush
sounds closer on the last drop of hill
where the walls of a gorge lean together
to make a sort of cave, its darkness
deep enough to hold a colony
of guachero birds, flyers in darkness,
whose fat lit Carib and Arawak lamps.

Our flashlights glitter the eyes of birds,
coals burning in darkness, ancient memories
of native people who harvested them,
yet never took more than they needed,
never bulldozed earth to bleed red into seas
stained by the waste of lives not yet named.

At the edge of the gorge, stepping on wet stones,
our balance uneasy, we come from darkness.
By the stream, the skull and a single femur
of an agouti glistens with the sun.
Washed here by high waters, white as paper,
I want to speak what these bones tell,
what the roots of trees, hanging down from the cliff,
a half woven veil seeking lodgement in air
might say to a northern world which seems
to value only fiscal balance.

As we climb the slope, I try to remember
the colors and calls of a hundred birds
I never saw wild before this morning,
so much I want only to leave behind,
undisturbed as the air which holds their flight,
which fills their lungs as well as my own,
a sharing that I pray may last
uncounted generations to come.

THE TIGER SALAMANDER

Spots smooth as the circles
formed by rain on the pond,
it came up in the mesh,
mud breaking from its shoulders,
mouth open as if to the first backboned breath.

Its black anthracite gleam
around housepaint white patterns
held all of the eyes in the Vertebrate class
that had looked with disinterest
on shocked sticklebacks from Six Mile Creek
and speckled hawk's eggs shinnied down from the oak.

When, like everything else
we found that day,
we placed the salamander
back into the sink hole
one boy from the city
who'd driven his Buick
to the marsh went back,
dipped for twenty minutes,
wire net like a tennis racket
dripped weeds into a pile
which grew up to his knees
till he found it again,
to take back to his frat.
He kept it till summer,
forgot it and left it
to a fading dry death.

That wet spring morning,
it looked up at us,
one leg poised, mouth open,
colors bright as the texture of legend
stepping out of an older dream,
wanting to own nothing
but itself.

SNAPPING TURTLE ON THE EXPRESSWAY

For Ron Welburn

Back ridged, ancient as a walking rock,
the turtle moved, step by stalking step,
across the double lane as cars
and trucks slowed to avoid its bulk.

It hissed as if its breath were hard
out of water's embrace, shell lifted up
the full length of its legs,
awkward on land, yet strong enough
to move with the power
of dream or vision,
like the steps of the pau-waus,
the tent-shaking seers
who emerged to light
after diving down deep
to hear healing songs.

A Greyhound bus braked, swerved over,
a dinosaur of blue metal, less sure
of its right of way than the turtle,
holder of Earth in longhouse stories.

You spoke of it over the phone,
how it reached the median and then,
without pause, headed out again,
across the northbound lane this time
to some pond memory said was there
even after roads cut the centuries
of trails remembered by a brain
too primitive to forget.
You knew you did not see it hit.

You prayed that it went on, survived,
its slow certainty something we
have learned to celebrate in our lives.

SEEING THE WHALES

1.

Great Life, the Mohawk people call
the whale, its motion through the sea
gentle and slow as the surge of tide,
strong as the push of wave against beach.

Within the boat, we watch the backs
of Humpback whales and Finback whales.
We watch their breath—a lifting cloud
where horizon and level sea are one.

Where their tails surge up as they swim
clear water makes a footprint shape
and when the Humpbacks dive, they lift
their tails as if to wave farewell,
showing a pattern black and white,
the tails of no two whales the same.

2.

Humpbacks, when they dive
feeding on small fish
weave nets of bubbles
circling closer till
they swim through, scooping
great mouthfuls, building
layers of blubber
for their fall trek back
to southern waters.

They sing as they swim,
and the Finback's song
is so low, so deep
microphones catch it
fifty miles away.
According to some
scientists, their songs
once carried half a
thousand miles before
our throbbing engines
broke the ancient web.

Some of them are scarred
where giant ships cut
across them as they
lifted to surfaces
trusting that ancient
safety of the high sea
still was their own.

3.

Just when we think we've seen the last,
one finds us as we seek them.
A huge Humpback, it comes straight up
to our boat, rolls, turns on its side
to wave green flippers as we watch.
It lifts to focus one great eye,
breath from its blowhole misting faces.
It stays there longer than we can,
looking at us as if with that
same wonder our eyes hold for it,
the ocean's grandeur turned to flesh.

But we must leave, for others wait
this boat to visit these last whales,
these great ones we once knew in tales,
who carried Gluskap through the waves,
who smoke the pipe he gave in thanks.

Our boat gains speed, the Humpback's shape
flows and recedes into distance.
Spray from its blowhole punctuates
our small horizon, touches us
more than words or moving pictures.
Some here may never look again
at sea in that same easy way.
Some of us wonder now just what
it is we share, what it is we change.

DANCING CIRCLES
IN THE BEARPAWS

For my friends at Stone Child College

Pat Chief Stick pointed
our eyes to the hill.
Up there is where
we used to hear
the Little People.
Right up on top
there used to be
two rings.
Sometimes at night
we would hear them talking.
They haven't been heard
there for years
but one of them
was heard singing
just last spring.

The elders' voices
are filled with pain and love
as they pray in Cree
for everyone, but especially
for the children
tempted by drugs and alcohol.
When just one person dies
it is felt by us all,
it is felt so hard
that we never get over it.
Only a few here
have lived to be old
and so their voices
must be more strong.

Later, as the drum
plays a friendship song,
we join our hands
to the circling dance
a circle like
the arms of mountains
a circle like
the Great Bear's embrace
a circle like the sun
which dances above us
a circle like the
willow sweat lodges
near the creeks
where beavers dam the water
and mountain trout
dart bright as dreams.

So we dance one more circle
and we share the breath
of these mountains in
a dance which may carry
our children into another century.
We dance our hearts into
the earth which loves us
as much as we care for it.
We dance for our elders
and for the grandchildren.
We dance slow and strong
for those after us
whose steps must begin
where ours end
and in this same circle
will dance, will dance
where our feet have been.

FOREST FIRE FROM THE AIR

At first my eyes focus
on the yellow curves
of highway lights strong
among dark mountain flanks
like the phosphorescent marks
outlining the bodies of deepsea fish.
Then I see it, feel its deeper color,
like blood flowing from a long wound,
a seam of earth opened to ancient magma,
the sinew of trees that stitched it together
swirling up, pluming a great pale feather
over the dark hills of Carter County.

Fire on the mountain—not a fiddle tune
or an I Ching symbol omening trouble,
but an ideogram written by the frustration
of small men with gasoline and matches.
In this dry fall of the heart,
the lights of arson are confused sentences
scrawled on the autumn lands
with brushstrokes of flame.

MEDICINE BUNDLES

I was taken once
into the basement
of a museum
in South Dakota.
There, within a tray
was a medicine bundle
but I didn't pick it up
or touch it.
I knew
I did not know enough.

I tell this story to my sons.
Imagine a man
who is shown a gun,
a man who has never
seen a gun before.
He lifts it up,
hefts its weight
in his hand, spins
the cylinder,
likes the feel of it,
points it in
a certain direction
and then his finger
finds the trigger. . . .

I was taken once
into a basement
in a museum in South Dakota.
In a drawer
was a medicine bundle,
but when the curator
picked it, and hefted it
and offered it
to me
I did not take it
in my hands.

ROUTINE CHECK

Late winter snow
feathers the sky
as a voice on the line
from some place
I have never been
asks me if I remember
who called my number
from Des Moines, Iowa
on the 17th of September

I don't know anyone
in Des Moines,
but then, disembodied,
that business-like voice
suggests the caller
may have been
an Indian
from Rosebud, South Dakota

Leonard Crow Dog,
I think,
but before I can speak
I am asked this question:
By any chance,
do I belong
to their religion?
What religion is that?
You know,
the Sun Dance.

May I ask, I ask
what this is for?

Just a routine check,
just a routine check,
just a routine check
on a credit card number.

Late winter snow
falls on the Paha Sapa,
the sacred Black Hills
which know no religion,
which cannot be owned
like credit card numbers.

There, routine checks
at Pine Ridge and Rosebud
turn up Indians,
snow in open mouths,
government bullets
in their backs.

There, at roadblocks
manned by BIA ghosts
voices ask
in that efficient tone
neutral as white paper,
Do you belong?

They receive no answer,
only the wind,
the spirit of Crazy Horse
thrusting his pony
against the snow,
believing in spring.

LET THE MIDNIGHT SPECIAL

In this year of executioners' songs,
another music stirs my memory,
a part of that time when we
lived in flowered dreams
as Credence sang, rough-voiced
as a southern spring:
Let the Midnight Special
shine its light on me.

Remember the story of how that song
was composed in a prison
where the moonshine beam
of a late freight would cut
across walls
as men held out their hands

knowing that if
that brilliance
touched them
they'd go free.

Today
the tracks
curve further away
and names are buried under stone.

Will their bones
make the mortar stronger
as each mile of the Great Wall
of China, built to keep barbarians out,
was reinforced with peasants' blood?

Astronauts say
that of all we have made
that ambling line
of futile stone
is the clearest thing seen
by an eye far out in space.

Its long shadow is clear
as iron rails
touched by moon's reflecting light.

Who is riding
that train tonight?

GROSS NATIONAL PRODUCT

The Corner of Howard and Seventh

1.

A flurry of motion
& across the street
3 young bums converge
and lift tenderly
up from pavement
the head of the old man
who jerked and collapsed,
a string-cut puppet.

They hold his coat,
bag, stocking cap,
feel his face,
his forehead,
then prop him up,
an overweight
and floppy doll,
legs straight
out like
a stretching athlete.

A black man
on my side of the street
seeing me watching says
"He'll be all right.
Jes had onea them
alcoholic seizures.
They just got
to get him cross the street,
that's the detox center."

2.

I round the corner
and piles of trash
resolve themselves
into Indian faces—
four men and
one woman embraced
by bulky rags,
nodding off—
Sunday afternoon wine
like feed sacks
piled together.

The youngest one smiles,
"Hey, what is it, Brother?"
as I pass,
the five of them
huddled so close,
camped out
on their Mission corner,
a block from the new
Convention Center,
this dream
their village
concrete trees
at their backs.

3.

The parking lot
by the Greyhound Station
throbs like a feathered heart
with the wings
of five hundred pigeons
as they scurry after
the sweep of feed
flung from the hands
of an old woman in white,
bent like a comma
over her paper bag
as she sows
her grain
on the surface.

A worn man
with a smile on his face
wearing a torn
green Vietnam jacket
comes up to her,
wading ankle deep
through oblivious birds
bobbing their heads.

As he speaks to her
she turns her back,
clutching her side.
I hear her say,
"Only for the birds!"
& he pats her shoulder,
laughs
and walks away.

BEFORE THE QUAKE:
FOUR IMAGES IN SAN FRANCISCO

1.

Father Serra's concrete ghost
stands larger than life,
his flesh now as hard
as the stone of the missions
mortared with Ohlone Indian blood.
On the kneeling hillside
above the highway
which bears his name
he points with one finger
towards the west,
the direction of the unquiet ocean,
the direction of the setting sun,
the direction of that hidden line
where another fault with
a holy man's name
waits like a long mouth
ready to open
and close over highways
and other monuments
to a simple American faith.

2.

In Berkeley, the boys
from the Beta House
beat up last week
ten brown-skinned students.

The graduate assistant
with a horse's grace
tells me, her Sioux accent soft,
she cannot talk with us after class
it's a long way home
across this enemy land
they call a college campus.

In the dark she sees hiding in the bushes
the white faces of hostile natives,
their anger stirred by obsidian hair.

3.

The windows have been
put back again
in the bank at Berkeley
where bricks were filled in
against the 1970's anger
at the death and waste
of Indochina.

Now, with new
enemies in the news,
money still drains
from the veins of this land
to pump the dry hearts
of weapons factories.

Old lines redrawn,
just the names are changed.
And in the last few days
each one of those windows
has been broken.

4.

In the People's Park in the Mission District
a hundred dark men circle trash can fires.
Laughter turns as new cars cruise by,
heavy-bodied fish in a sea washed by hunger.
They are other fires beneath this concrete,
there are older fires in their eyes.

BLUE COYOTE

Sonora

First Maker walked
and where he went
each step became a living thing.
He walked through thorns,
left horned lizards behind,
walked through colored sands,
Gila monsters were there.

With a piece of flint
on the cliff of blue stone
he drew a shape—
lean with four legs,
a head always looking
back over its shoulder,
its tail a breathing wind.

Then, quick as an arrow
released from a bow,
it leaped from the cliff
right up into the heavens.

Now, when night sky is clear,
do you have to ask
whose bright eyes
look down into your dreams?

THE FIRST HORSE

For Swift Eagle

When Killer of Enemies
lived up there
in that upper world above the clouds,
he dreamt the first horse,
then singing, singing, singing each part,
made the horse from his dream.
From the cornstalk he shaped
the spine and the legs,
from the foam on the waters
after heavy rain
he shaped the lungs,
singing he did this,
singing he did this,
singing he did this, singing.
He gathered the hailstones
to make the liver,
took shining hailstones
to make the teeth.
He caught a bolt of lightning
and then fastened that lightning
within the nostrils,
to give that horse of his
fiery breath.
Singing he did this,
singing he did this,
singing he did this, singing.
Then he searched the heavens
to finish his work.
From the crescent moon
he shaped the ears,
he took the Evening Star
from the sky and shaped
a piece of it into the eyes.
Now that horse could see
in both day and night.

Singing he did this,
singing he did this,
singing he did this, singing.

Then the time came
to give his creation life.
He gathered the whirlwinds
in his hands, one from each
of the four directions.
The one from the west
went beneath the shoulders,
the one from the east
went into the flanks,
and those remaining
from north and south
went into the horse's mighty hips.
Singing he did this,
singing he did this,
singing he did this, singing.

Then, reaching up, he gathered the comet
and shaped the sweep of his horse's tail.
Now that horse began to move and breathe,
now Killer of Enemies had his steed.
Singing he did this,
singing he did this,
singing he did this, singing.

Last of all, he shaped
his horse's saddle.
His saddle blanket
was a cirrus cloud,
his buckle, the moon,
saddle horn the sun
and the cinch beneath
the belly was the rainbow.
Then, singing, singing,
singing, singing, he rode.

RAVEN STORY

Fairbanks, Alaska

The voices in the wind
are talking, talking, talking,
they speak of Raven
for Raven, too, is
always talking,
looking down
from the crest of cedar

The cannibal giant's
heart was hidden
within his heel
it was Raven
who saw that

Listen you people
he called down to them
just as these birds
call down to us
from their height above
the cars which circle
their slow morning way
into the university

Listen, he said,
that's the place to kill it,
right down there, strike hard
at that place with your spears
do that and no longer
will it kill your people

That time they listened
The monster was killed
its heel pierced by their spears
but the people said
let's be really sure
let's burn it up

From the top of the tree
Raven shook his head
he called to warn them
Don't do it, he said
as he looked down
from his tall tree
above Prince William Sound
as the tanker edged
its way towards the reef

But all they heard then
all they hear now
was his bird voice
they didn't hear words
and the smoke rose up
thick from their fire
and turned into
thirsty blood-sucking mosquitoes

They did not listen
and the air grew thick
with clouds of mosquitoes
and the sea flowed black

And Raven keeps talking
talking, talking, always talking
from the crest of the cedar

and who is listening?

INUPIAQ—THE WHALERS

I.

In April when
the Open Lead, that break in the ice
which becomes the whale road,
appears beyond the iceheld shores,
Inupiaq boats of wood and walrus hide
take to the water
drawn once more
by their old bond of blood.

II.

Tommy's grandfather taught him
the place to strike,
that small indentation
just behind the whale's head.
He was seventeen, on his first hunt.
The chosen whale his uncles struck
kept swimming, swimming,
towing their umiak
and refusing to die
even when they lanced it
again and again in the side.
Tommy knew it was suffering.

You're doing it wrong.
I know how to kill it.
Give me the harpoon, he said.
His uncle stared at him,
then picked up the lance,
held it out at arm's length
so the point touched his face.

Tommy leaped from the boat,
up onto the whale's back
and began to walk, water
streaming over his feet,
then washing up as deep as his waist
as the wounded bowhead surged
through the waves.
When he found the spot,
he said a quick prayer,
I am sorry my brother
to have caused you such pain.
Then he lifted the lance,
drove it in without pausing,
pushed it in deep
at the base of the neck
drove it down hard
till it cut through the spine.
The whole whale quivered
beneath his feet, then
grew still as it died.

III.

The old man, his eyes
ranging over the pack ice,
told me how his father
taught him to know the whale.
He was very small then
and the men had pulled
the bowhead up onto the ice.

I want you to touch
every inch of that whale
just as long at it takes,
you take your time.

He spent the rest
of that morning then,
walking around it,
drawing his hands
down the length of its side,
crawling onto its flukes,
placing his small fingers
in the great open eyes.
That night he dreamt
that he swam beneath ice.

Today, as he holds
the bone in his hands,
shaping a diving whale
with his knife,
he knows the way
to find its life.

IV.

On Saint Lawrence Island
when our whale is brought out,
Grace Slwooko said,
and we cut it up,
we must lay its body
there on the ice
in the same shape
it had when it
still was alive.

That way, when its brothers
and sisters look up
from beneath they'll see
that it isn't so bad
to give themselves to us
when we keep them
whole in that way,
whole in our hearts.

V.

The Point Hope whaling captain gestured—
you see the way that fog moves in,
above the ice? It is always that way,
it is always grey in the whaling season.

When the Great Spirit made the whale
he made it his most perfect creation.
But then he saw the Inupiaq,
we needed to hunt the whale to live.

So he said, I give you people permission
to kill the bowhead, my best creature.
But only now, just this time of year,
when I'll send the fog for I
do not have to see them die.

CROSSING INTO WEST GERMANY

1989

There are borders on earth
and lines on the maps,
colors and barriers, human names
stuck onto the soil, as if earth could claim
to understand or speak our tongues,
as if the hawks looking down in long flight
saw nations and flags, not forests and valleys,
places to live, to hunt, care for their young.

But the wind still blows
over every border
and the soil that sifts
through the hands of farmers
responds the same
to drought and rain.

Ask me now
to which nation
I belong
and I will answer
without words in a song,
that language all
our ancestors spoke,
learned from the flow
of clear streams to the sea,
birds chanting praise
to each dawn.

ALTAMIRA

Black silence
then the hiss of fire,
scrape of rough pigment
rich as blood with iron.

The bison, the horses
hold in midstride,
caught by the eye,
the line of the spear
piercing their flanks.

What happens then,
as ten thousand leaf-falls
flicker like faces
past the window of stone?

Some of us think
in a world cooling quicker
than hot steel thrust in water
while smoke lifts,
dims the stars,
that the animals wait.

They were meant
more than magic to make the hunt good
or a spirit's placation,
to be like those seeds
which the centuries hold
in dry hands till the rain
brings forth an answer
to warmth and the sun.

There's still space on the dream wall.
Let us hold up our torches.

THE BAUX

Provence, France

The wind across the Alpillines
was dry with heat and the earth of the Baux
crumbled under our feet.
"Eagles Ever, Servants Never,"
that was the motto of those harsh lords
of this high-cragged city fort,
all of Provence held under their eyes.
The millenial winds and the hands of men
carved the stones of the hills
into figures of fear and it was for
the dark deeds of men
that the vale below
became known as the Valley of Evil.

Today, the small streets of a tourist town
wind up through a city of the dead.
Now only the wind walks here at night
above rocks bone-white as the fingers
of a long-clenched fist, cleansed
by death of both greed and flesh.
The brow of the hill where armies gathered
is open and empty as a skull's eye sockets,
empty of all ambition and vision.

Small flowers grow here.
Matthew, whose ancestors
served those lords, points them out to me.
They are there at our feet,
yellow, blue and white
as they were before we came.
They are always in blossom
among the dry stones,
finding moisture in crevices,
drawing life from this light
that blinds most human eyes.

ST. FRANCIS AND THE WOLF

When St. Francis walked out
from the city's walls,
the grey of dawn was at his back
along with those less filled with faith
who followed, yet hung back to flee,
less certain than one
who allowed no protection
other than his praise
of all God's Creation.

The wolf came from the forest,
heavy-shouldered, head down.
Though men called him cruel
he carried their wounds.
He had seen his young
smoked out of their den,
watched his mate fall
to the crossbow's bolt.

When St. Francis looked
into the wolf's eyes
he knew they were
not the color of hell
nor the crimson of blood,
but filled instead
with the flame of freedom,
bright as the rising sun.
He placed his hands
on the great wolf's head
as another man
might caress a chalice.

"Brother Wolf," said Francis
in a voice which sang
like the forest's own depths,
"You have not done well
to frighten these people.
I know you've done no wrong.
Your flesh and mine
are the same, my brother.
No more will people hate you
from within the walls of Gubbio."

St. Francis returned
with the wolf by his side.
"Let this brother of mine,"
he said to the people,
"pass freely through
the streets of your city.
Keep faith with his freedom
and his love will last
longer than the walls of your town,
as long as the streams
which both wolves and men
watch with wonder
still carry the rain
from the hills into the sea."

TURNING FROM THE KLAN

The memory began
when a friend of my son's
suggested they should go
to a costume party
as Ku Klux Klansmen . . .

A summer night in Mississippi
and I cannot remember the sounds of the frogs
singing from the ditches beside those roads.

I only remember the pain in my feet
after walking twenty miles and more that day
with Stokely Carmichael and Martin Luther King,
James Meredith and young Jesse Jackson.
I remember the crickets or was it just the sound,
the clicking mechanical sound of the cameras,
the Polaroids held by the southern patrolmen
as they took all our pictures, showing them
to each other, then smiling and nodding
and whispering—*See you later* . . .

And I remember that we were lost, halfway
on the road to that church in Jackson
where we were to sleep that night on the floor.
There were six of us in that rented car,
a white driver from Philadelphia,
three black South Africans, myself
and Inge, from Sweden, whose long
blonde hair swung round her face like
a semaphore as she sat in front
by the open window.
And I remember that close behind us,
was a station wagon filled
with thick-necked white men.
The dome light was on
and their faces glowed
like jack-o-lanterns
as if lit from within,
and their hands
were out of sight.

They followed us
for ten miles that night
as we kept to the streets
where the lights were brightest
until, at last, in desperation
we turned down the one
shaded lane I remembered
which took us towards
the black side of town,
a haven from their white light.
The wagon behind us
melted away, the white robes
and flushed faces vanished—
though some of them would reappear
beneath the hats of Mississippi
state troopers next day by the line of march.
But the rest of that night, the night
was dark and safe around us.

My young son refused to wear those robes,
even as a joke, without knowing this story
which I never told him, which might have been
the tale of how he might not have been
had we taken a turn towards the edge of the town
where the sounds of frogs and crickets were loud,
almost as loud as the firecracker pop
of shotguns heard from miles away
and louder than the small splash of bodies
weighted to sink into southern mud.

Instead, we turned,
turned the right way
and each of us holds a memory
as years become decades
and the long march goes on
as a son refuses,
knowing without knowing why.